CHAPTER 1: INTRODUCT

Understanding the Fascinating World of Scorpions

Scorpions, with their striking appearance and ancient lineage, represent a remarkable and diverse group of arachnids that have roamed the Earth for millions of years. This chapter offers a comprehensive exploration into the intricate world of scorpions, shedding light on their intricate anatomy, intriguing ecological adaptations, and captivating behavioral patterns. Delve into the following aspects to develop a profound understanding of the captivating world of scorpions:

Anatomical Features: Embark on an exploration of the unique anatomical features that define scorpions. From their characteristic segmented exoskeleton and sensory pincers to their powerful stingers and venom-injecting tails, each aspect of their anatomy serves a critical purpose in their survival, ranging from hunting and defense to sensory perception and reproduction.

Ecological Diversity: Journey through the

diverse habitats and ecosystems that scorpions call home, spanning a vast range of geographical locations and environmental conditions worldwide. Explore their adaptive strategies for thriving in various landscapes, from the harsh and arid deserts of North Africa and the Middle East to the humid tropical rainforests of Southeast Asia and the grassy plains of North America.

Behavioral Patterns: Uncover the intricacies of scorpion behavior, from their nocturnal hunting rituals and unique locomotion methods to their complex mating dances and social interactions within their colonies. Gain insights into their well-honed sensory abilities, including their acute detection of vibrations, pheromones, and ambient temperature changes, which contribute to their adept navigation and survival in their often-challenging habitats.

Exploring the Diversity of Scorpion Species and Habitats Embark on an in-depth exploration of the rich and diverse tapestry of scorpion species that inhabit various corners of the globe. Discover the multitude of morphological adaptations, ranging from the size and shape of their pincers to the coloration and venom potency, which are tailored to their specific habitats and evolutionary histories. Gain a deeper understanding of their roles within their ecosystems, including their predation on insects, their contribution to nutrient cycling, and their significance as both predator and prey in the intricate web of desert and tropical food chains.

Delve into the intricate relationships between scorpions and their environments, including their interactions with other organisms, their responses to climatic fluctuations, and their reliance on specific microhabitats for shelter and protection. By immersing yourself in the detailed exploration of scorpion diversity and ecological adaptations, you can develop a profound appreciation for the intricate balance and interdependence that characterizes the captivating world of scorpions.

CHAPTER 2: SETTING UP THE IDEAL SCORPION HABITAT

Creating a Suitable Enclosure for Your Scorpion

The foundation of responsible scorpion care begins with providing an optimal habitat that replicates their natural environment and meets their specific needs. This chapter delves into the critical considerations for setting up the perfect enclosure to ensure your scorpion's well-being and comfort. Explore the following aspects to create a secure and comfortable habitat for your scorpion:

Enclosure Selection: Choose an enclosure that suits the size and behavior of your scorpion species. Consider options such as glass terrariums, plastic containers, or acrylic enclosures, ensuring they offer adequate ventilation and are escape-proof.

Substrate Selection: Select an appropriate substrate that mimics your scorpion's native habitat. Common substrates include sand, coconut coir, or a mix of both to provide a stable and burrowable medium. Ensure the substrate is deep enough for burrowing species and maintains the desired moisture level.

Temperature and Lighting: Establish a temperature gradient within the enclosure, with a warm side and a cooler side to accommodate your scorpion's thermoregulation needs. Utilize under-tank heaters or heat mats to maintain stable temperature ranges. While most scorpions are nocturnal and don't require UVB lighting, providing low-intensity ambient lighting can create a natural day-night cycle.

Choosing the Appropriate Substrate and Decor for a Comfortable Environment

Substrate Depth: Depending on your scorpion species, provide a substrate depth suitable for burrowing. Species like Hadrurus arizonensis may require several inches of substrate for burrowing and creating shelters. Shallow substrates are more appropriate for species that prefer surface dwelling.

Hiding Spots: Incorporate natural or artificial

shelters like cork bark, half logs, or coconut hides within the enclosure. These hiding spots offer a sense of security for your scorpion and mimic the crevices they would seek in the wild.

Environmental Enrichment: Enhance the enclosure with elements such as rocks, small branches, or leaf litter to create a visually stimulating environment. Scorpions may use these elements for hunting, climbing, or web construction, enriching their behavioral repertoire.

Hydration: Provide a shallow water dish with clean, dechlorinated water for scorpions to drink from and maintain proper humidity levels. Avoid deep water dishes to prevent accidental drowning.

By carefully crafting an enclosure that mirrors the natural conditions your scorpion would encounter in the wild, you not only ensure their physical well-being but also create an enriching environment that allows them to exhibit their natural behaviors and thrive in captivity.

CHAPTER 3: TEMPERATURE AND HUMIDITY MANAGEMENT

Maintaining Optimal Temperature and Humidity Levels for Scorpion Health

Temperature and humidity are critical factors in ensuring the health and well-being of your scorpion. This chapter delves into the importance of maintaining these parameters, offering insights into the ideal conditions for different scorpion species and strategies to achieve them. Explore the following aspects to provide a comfortable and healthy environment for your scorpion:

Optimal Temperature Ranges: Understanding the temperature preferences of your scorpion species is crucial. While most scorpions are mesothermal, meaning they require moderate temperatures, specific species may have varying requirements. Establish a temperature gradient within the enclosure, offering a warm area (around 80-90°F) and a cooler area (around 70-80°F) to allow your scorpion to regulate its body temperature.

Heating Solutions: Utilize appropriate heating methods to achieve and maintain the desired temperature ranges. Under-tank heating pads, heat tape, or heat cables placed under one side of the enclosure are effective options. Employ thermostats to ensure precise temperature control and prevent overheating.

Implementing Effective Heating and Moisture Control Strategies

Ambient Humidity: Research the humidity requirements of your scorpion species. While many scorpions are adapted to arid environments, some, like rainforest species, require higher humidity levels. Ensure adequate ventilation while misting the enclosure as needed or adding a moist substrate to create a suitable humidity level.

Humidity Monitoring: Regularly monitor humidity levels using a hygrometer to ensure they remain within the appropriate range. Adjust misting or substrate moisture accordingly to maintain stable humidity conditions.

Substrate Moisture: For scorpions that require higher humidity, a moist substrate can be beneficial. Maintain a layer of moist substrate in one area of the enclosure to provide a microclimate with increased humidity.

Moisture Retreats: Create designated moisture retreats within the enclosure, such as cork bark hides with damp sphagnum moss, to offer your scorpion a location to access moisture when needed.

Ventilation: Ensure proper ventilation to prevent stagnant air and mold growth. Screen tops or well-ventilated enclosures help to maintain good air circulation.

By mastering temperature and humidity management and tailoring these parameters to the specific needs of your scorpion species, you ensure that your scorpion's physiological processes, metabolic activity, and overall health remain in optimal condition.

CHAPTER 4: FEEDING AND NUTRITION

Exploring the Dietary Preferences and Requirements of Scorpions

Feeding is a fundamental aspect of scorpion care that directly impacts their health and vitality. This chapter delves into the intriguing world of scorpion feeding habits, their dietary preferences, and the essential considerations for providing a well-balanced and nutritious diet. Explore the following aspects to promote the well-being of your scorpion through proper nutrition:

Dietary Preferences: Scorpions are carnivorous predators that primarily feed on live prey. Delve into the dietary preferences of your scorpion species, ranging from insects and arachnids to other small invertebrates. Some scorpions may exhibit specific preferences for certain types of prey, reflecting their natural hunting behaviors.

Feeding Frequency: Determine the appropriate feeding frequency for your scorpion. While some species may require regular meals, others are adapted to survive on sporadic feeding. Understanding the metabolic needs of your scorpion helps establish an appropriate feeding schedule.

Live Prey Selection: Identify and select suitable live prey items based on your scorpion's size and preferences. Common prey options include crickets, roaches, mealworms, and small arachnids. Ensure that prey items are of an appropriate size, and monitor your scorpion's feeding response to adjust prey selection as needed.

Tips for Providing a Nutrient-Rich Diet to Promote Vitality and Well-Being

Gut Loading: Consider gut loading prey items with nutrient-rich foods before offering them to your scorpion. This practice enhances the nutritional value of the prey, ensuring your scorpion receives a balanced diet.

Supplementation: Depending on the species, you may need to provide additional supplements to bolster the nutritional content of your scorpion's diet. Consult with experts or conduct research to determine the specific supplementation requirements of your scorpion species.

Observation: Regularly monitor your scorpion during feeding to ensure it captures and consumes its prey. Remove uneaten prey items promptly to prevent injury to your scorpion and maintain a clean enclosure.

Hydration: Remember that scorpions obtain some of their hydration from their prey. Ensure that your scorpion receives access to clean, dechlorinated water to supplement its hydration needs.

By exploring the dietary preferences and requirements of your scorpion and implementing appropriate feeding strategies, you can promote their vitality and overall well-being. Tailoring their diet to mimic their natural foraging habits and providing the necessary nutrients ensures that your scorpion remains healthy and thriving in captivity.

CHAPTER 5: HANDLING AND INTERACTION

Safe and Responsible Handling Practices for Scorpion Enthusiasts

While the primary focus of scorpion keeping is observation and care from a distance, there may be instances where handling becomes necessary or desired. This chapter explores the guidelines for safe and responsible scorpion handling and interaction. Discover the following aspects to ensure the well-being of both you and your scorpion:

Handling Precautions: Understand the importance of handling precautions to minimize the risk of envenomation or harm. Wearing protective clothing like gloves, long sleeves, and eye protection can provide a safety barrier.

Species-Specific Considerations: Different scorpion species have varying temperaments and venom potencies. Research the behavior of your specific scorpion species to gauge its suitability for handling. Some species are more docile, while others may be prone to defensive behaviors.

Taming and Habituation: If you wish to handle your scorpion, invest time in taming and habituating it to human contact. Gradual and gentle interactions can help your scorpion become accustomed to handling and reduce its stress response.

Understanding the Behavior and Temperament of Scorpions for Safe Interaction

Behavioral Cues: Learn to interpret the behavioral cues of your scorpion, such as its posture, tail position, and responsiveness. Recognizing signs of agitation or stress can help you gauge when it's not an appropriate time for handling.

Timing: Choose the right time for handling, which is typically during your scorpion's active period, usually at night for most species. Avoid interrupting your scorpion during its resting phase to minimize stress.

Gentle Handling Techniques: Master gentle handling techniques, such as using soft brushes or cups, to encourage your scorpion to climb onto your hand. Avoid sudden movements or disturbances that can startle or provoke your scorpion.

Supervision: Always handle your scorpion with supervision, especially if you're new to scorpion keeping or working with a potentially defensive species. Having a responsible person nearby can offer assistance in case of unexpected reactions.

Safety should always be the top priority when handling scorpions. Remember that, in general, scorpions are best observed within their enclosure, where they can exhibit their natural behaviors without undue stress or risk to their well-being. If handling is necessary, approach it with caution, knowledge, and respect for your scorpion's comfort and safety.

CHAPTER 6: HEALTH AND
DISEASE MANAGEMENT

Identifying Common Health Issues and Ailments in Scorpions

Maintaining the health and well-being of your scorpion is paramount in ensuring its longevity and vitality. This chapter delves into the essential knowledge and practices for identifying common health issues and ailments that may affect your scorpion. Explore the following aspects to recognize signs of potential health concerns and promote early intervention:

Symptoms of Illness: Familiarize yourself with the common symptoms of illness in scorpions, such as lethargy, loss of appetite, abnormal behavior, limb abnormalities, or changes in exoskeleton appearance. Understanding these indicators can help you identify potential health issues early on.

Parasitic Infestations: Be vigilant for signs of parasitic infestations, such as mites or ticks, that may affect your scorpion's well-being. Regularly inspect your scorpion and its enclosure for any signs of external parasites, and take prompt measures to eliminate them.

Fungal and Bacterial Infections: Be aware of the signs of fungal or bacterial infections, such as discoloration, lesions, or abnormal growths on the exoskeleton. Maintain a clean and hygienic enclosure to minimize the risk of such infections and ensure proper ventilation to prevent the buildup of moisture.

Implementing Preventative Measures and Treatment Protocols for a Healthy Scorpion

Hygienic Practices: Establish a regular cleaning and maintenance routine for your scorpion's enclosure, including substrate changes, removal of uneaten prey, and spot cleaning to prevent the accumulation of waste and potential pathogens.

Quarantine Protocols: Introduce new scorpions to your collection through a quarantine period to prevent the spread of potential diseases to your existing scorpions. Observe new arrivals for any signs of illness before integrating them into the main enclosure.

Veterinary Consultation: Establish a relationship with a veterinarian experienced in arachnid care to seek professional guidance and treatment if you suspect your scorpion is unwell. Consult with them for preventative care recommendations and regular check-ups to ensure your scorpion's ongoing health.

By vigilantly monitoring your scorpion's health, implementing preventative measures, and seeking timely veterinary care when necessary, you can ensure that your scorpion remains resilient and robust, capable of thriving in its captive environment.

CHAPTER 7: SOCIAL DYNAMICS
AND TANK MATES

Understanding Scorpion Behavior in Group Settings

While scorpions are typically solitary creatures, understanding their social dynamics and the potential for communal living is crucial for creating a harmonious scorpion community. This chapter explores the complexities of scorpion behavior in group settings and offers insights into the considerations for introducing tank mates. Discover the following aspects to foster a safe and comfortable social environment for your scorpion:

Solitary Nature: Understand that most scorpions are solitary by nature and prefer to live and hunt alone. Recognize the potential stress and conflicts that can arise from forced social interactions or overcrowding within an enclosure.

Group Behavior Observations: Conduct thorough observations of scorpion behavior in group settings, if applicable, to gauge their tolerance for communal living. Look for signs of aggression, territoriality, or stress, and be prepared to separate individuals if necessary.

Selecting Suitable Tank Mates and Managing Interactions for a Harmonious Scorpion Community

Species Compatibility: Research species that are known to be compatible for communal living, if you intend to keep multiple scorpions together. Opt for species with similar size, temperament, and environmental requirements to minimize the risk of conflict or competition.

Enclosure Size: Provide an adequately sized enclosure that allows each scorpion to establish its territory and retreat to a separate space when needed. Ensure that there are ample hiding spots and resources to prevent competition for food and shelter.

Group Composition: Introduce tank mates simultaneously to prevent the establishment of territorial boundaries by one scorpion before the introduction of others. Monitor interactions closely during the initial phase of introduction to ensure a smooth and gradual acclimation process.

Monitoring and Intervention: Regularly monitor group interactions to identify any signs of aggression or stress. Be prepared to intervene and separate scorpions if conflicts escalate or if individuals display signs of distress.

Creating a harmonious scorpion community requires careful consideration of species compatibility, environmental enrichment, and vigilant monitoring of social interactions. While some scorpions may thrive in communal setups, others may exhibit territorial or aggressive behaviors that necessitate solitary housing. Prioritize the well-being and safety of your scorpion companions when considering their social dynamics and tank mate interactions.

CHAPTER 8: REPRODUCTION AND BREEDING

Insights into the Reproductive Process of Scorpions

Reproduction is a significant aspect of scorpion biology and behavior. This chapter delves into the fascinating world of scorpion reproduction, offering insights into their mating rituals, gestation, and the birth of offspring. Gain a deeper understanding of the reproductive process of scorpions through the following aspects:

Mating Rituals: Explore the intricate and often ritualistic courtship behaviors displayed by scorpions during the mating process. Learn about the exchange of pheromones, visual displays, and tactile interactions that precede copulation.

Copulation and Sperm Transfer: Understand the mechanics of copulation, including the transfer of sperm by the male to the female. Discover the role of specialized structures, such as the spermatophore, in this process.

Gestation and Brood Care: Delve into the

gestation period of scorpions, which can vary among species, and the subsequent care provided by the mother. Learn how female scorpions protect their developing offspring, often carrying them on their backs.

Nurturing and Rearing Offspring for a Successful Brood

Brood Size and Care: Gain insights into the variations in brood size and the maternal care provided by female scorpions. Understand how they defend and nurture their young during the early stages of development.

Molting and Dispersal: Discover the significance of molting for scorpion offspring as they grow and develop. Learn how young scorpions eventually disperse and embark on their solitary lives.

Breeding Challenges: Recognize the challenges and considerations associated with breeding scorpions in captivity, including temperature, humidity, and social dynamics. Explore strategies for overcoming obstacles and ensuring successful reproduction.

Understanding the reproductive process of scorpions is not only fascinating but also vital for those interested in breeding these arachnids. By gaining knowledge about their mating rituals, gestation, and brood care, you can appreciate the complexities of scorpion reproduction and make informed decisions when considering breeding in a captive setting.

CHAPTER 9: ADVANCED CARE
TECHNIQUES FOR ENTHUSIASTS

Fine-Tuning Habitat Parameters for Optimal Scorpion Well-Being

Achieving an advanced level of care for scorpions involves fine-tuning habitat parameters to meet their specific needs and promote their overall well-being. This chapter delves into the intricacies of advanced care techniques, offering insights into optimizing habitat conditions and implementing advanced strategies for a thriving scorpion habitat. Explore the following aspects to elevate your scorpion care to an advanced level:

Environmental Enrichment: Implement advanced environmental enrichment techniques, such as incorporating natural elements like live plants, rock formations, and artificial burrows within the enclosure. Create a dynamic and visually stimulating environment that encourages natural behaviors and promotes mental stimulation.

Photoperiod and Lighting: Fine-tune the

photoperiod and lighting within the enclosure to replicate natural day-night cycles and seasonal variations. Employ programmable lighting systems to create gradual transitions between day and night, mimicking the lighting conditions of your scorpion's native habitat.

Customized Feeding Regimens: Develop customized feeding regimens that cater to the specific dietary requirements and metabolic needs of your scorpion. Consider incorporating a variety of live prey items and supplements to ensure a well-balanced and nutrient-rich diet that supports optimal growth and vitality.

Implementing Advanced Techniques for a Thriving Scorpion Habitat

Temperature Regulation: Implement advanced temperature regulation techniques, such as creating localized temperature gradients and microclimates within the enclosure to accommodate the thermoregulatory needs of your scorpion. Utilize advanced heating and cooling systems, including ceramic heat emitters and misting systems, to maintain precise temperature ranges.

Humidity Control: Fine-tune humidity control within the enclosure by incorporating advanced misting systems, automated humidifiers, or fogging devices. Monitor and adjust humidity levels to match the specific requirements of your scorpion species, ensuring a stable and conducive microclimate for their physiological well-being.

Behavioral Observation and Enrichment: Engage in advanced behavioral observation and enrichment practices, such as conducting behavioral studies, documenting social interactions, and implementing cognitive enrichment tasks. Foster a deeper understanding of your scorpion's behavioral repertoire and cognitive abilities, and develop customized enrichment activities that promote mental stimulation and natural foraging behaviors.

Elevating your scorpion care to an advanced level involves a comprehensive understanding of their physiological, behavioral, and environmental requirements. By fine-tuning habitat parameters and implementing advanced care techniques, you can create an enriched and thriving environment that supports the overall well-being and natural behaviors of your scorpions.

CHAPTER 10: FREQUENTLY ASKED QUESTIONS (FAQS)

Q: How often should I feed my scorpion? A: The frequency of feeding varies depending on the species and age of your scorpion. Generally, offering appropriately sized live prey items once or twice a week is sufficient for adult scorpions, while younger scorpions may require more frequent feedings to support their growth.

Q: What should I do if my scorpion stops eating? A: A temporary loss of appetite can occur due to factors such as stress, environmental changes, or the molting process. Monitor your scorpion's behavior and ensure that the enclosure conditions are optimal. If the fasting period extends beyond a few weeks, consult with a reputable veterinarian or experienced scorpion keeper for further guidance.

Q: How can I tell if my scorpion is preparing to molt? A: Signs of an impending molt include reduced activity, loss of appetite, and a dulling of the exoskeleton.

Prior to molting, your scorpion may seek out a secure hiding spot to undergo the process. Ensure that the enclosure provides a suitable environment with adequate humidity and substrate depth to support a successful molt.

Q: What are the signs of a healthy scorpion? A: A healthy scorpion exhibits consistent feeding behavior, normal mobility, and a well-maintained exoskeleton. Clear and responsive sensory organs, along with intact and functional appendages, are also indicators of a healthy scorpion. Regularly monitor your scorpion for any signs of abnormal behavior or physical abnormalities.

Q: How can I create a suitable habitat for my scorpion? A: To create an ideal habitat, provide an appropriately sized enclosure with suitable substrate, temperature gradients, and hiding spots. Ensure that the enclosure is well-ventilated and offers the appropriate humidity levels for your scorpion species. Incorporate natural elements and environmental enrichment to encourage natural behaviors and promote mental stimulation.

Q: Can I house multiple scorpions together? A:

While some species may tolerate communal living, scorpions are typically solitary creatures that may exhibit territorial or aggressive behaviors when housed together. Conduct thorough research on species-specific behaviors and consider individual temperament and enclosure size before attempting to house multiple scorpions together.

Q: How do I handle my scorpion safely? A: When handling your scorpion, prioritize safety by wearing protective gear such as gloves and long sleeves. Approach your scorpion with gentle and deliberate movements, avoiding sudden actions that may startle or provoke it. Ensure that the handling session takes place in a calm and controlled environment, and be prepared to return your scorpion to its enclosure if it displays signs of agitation or stress.

Q: What should I do if my scorpion exhibits signs of illness or injury? A: If you notice any signs of illness or injury, such as lethargy, abnormal behavior, or physical abnormalities, consult with a knowledgeable veterinarian or experienced scorpion keeper immediately. Prompt intervention and appropriate medical care are essential to ensure the health and well-being of your scorpion.

Q: How can I promote natural behaviors in my scorpion? A: Promote natural behaviors by providing environmental enrichment, such as incorporating live plants, natural substrates, and appropriate hiding spots within the enclosure. Encourage foraging behaviors by offering live prey items that simulate hunting and capture activities. Implement behavioral observation practices to better understand your scorpion's behavioral repertoire and preferences.

Q: What are the essential components of a scorpion first aid kit? A: A scorpion first aid kit should include essential items such as sterile gauze, antiseptic solution, tweezers, and a safe container for temporary housing. Additionally, include contact information for a veterinarian experienced in treating scorpions and a comprehensive guide on handling and administering first aid to scorpions.

CHAPTER 11: CONCLUSION AND FINAL THOUGHTS

Recapitulating Essential Points for Successful Scorpion Care

Throughout this comprehensive guide, you have delved into the intricate world of scorpion care, exploring their unique behaviors, habitat requirements, and essential care practices. By emphasizing the significance of maintaining optimal habitat conditions, understanding their dietary needs, and fostering a safe and enriching environment, you have acquired valuable insights into providing exceptional care for your scorpion companions.

Key Takeaways:

Habitat Management: Establish and maintain an appropriate habitat that replicates the natural environment of your scorpion, ensuring optimal temperature, humidity, and environmental enrichment.

Dietary Considerations: Provide a well-balanced and nutrient-rich diet that caters to the specific dietary preferences and requirements of your scorpion, promoting their overall health and vitality.

Behavioral Understanding: Develop a deeper understanding of your scorpion's behavioral repertoire, fostering natural behaviors through environmental enrichment and attentive observation.

Encouragement and Inspiration for a Rewarding Journey with Scorpions

As you continue your journey in scorpion keeping, remember that patience, diligence, and a deep appreciation for these fascinating arachnids are essential. Embrace the opportunity to learn and grow alongside your scorpion companions, fostering a rewarding and fulfilling connection with these enigmatic creatures. Draw inspiration from the intricate marvels of their biology, behavior, and resilience, and let your passion for scorpions guide you on a path of continuous discovery and enrichment.

Your commitment to providing exceptional care for your scorpions contributes to their well-being and the preservation of their natural legacy. May your journey with scorpions be filled with wonder, learning, and the joy of nurturing these remarkable creatures.

Printed in Great Britain
by Amazon